THE LITTLE
BOOK FOR
CRYSTAL
LOVERS

ASTRID CARVEL

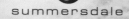

summersdale

THE LITTLE BOOK FOR CRYSTAL LOVERS

Copyright © Summersdale Publishers Ltd, 2022

Text by Susan McCann

An Hachette UK Company
www.hachette.co.uk

Summersdale Publishers Ltd
Part of Octopus Publishing Group Limited
Carmelite House
50 Victoria Embankment
LONDON
EC4Y 0DZ
UK

www.summersdale.com

Printed and bound in China

ISBN: 978-1-80007-643-3

Substantial discounts on bulk quantities of Summersdale books are available to corporations, professional associations and other organizations. For details contact general enquiries: telephone: +44 (0) 1243 771107 or email: enquiries@summersdale.com.

CONTENTS

INTRODUCTION

Crystals have been valued by mankind throughout time and are often used to heal trauma, protect against negative energy and treat ailments of both the mind and body. Conveniently, they also make beautiful jewellery and we love being adorned with them!

Just like us, crystals vibrate with energy, and when they're used in healing they balance the energies in the body, allowing for physical, mental or emotional healing. This vibrational medicine is something we can all benefit from – and best of all, it's something we can make use of ourselves simply by tuning into a crystal we hold in our hand, or which is placed on our body.

Crystals are easy to work with and choosing the right ones will help to bring balance and positivity into our lives. This guide explains the unique properties of 35 crystals and how to work with them, dividing them into seven useful categories to help with everything from stress to insomnia. This book also features birthstones for each month of the year, as well as offering simple tips on caring for your gems.

Not only are crystals beautiful but they can make a real difference to your life when used with dedication. Enjoy experimenting with these wise natural treasures!

A BRIEF HISTORY OF CRYSTALS

Like old friends, crystals have been with us forever – even before the known recording of time began. These natural fonts of knowledge and wisdom have become a part of our lives, helping us to heal as well as power our technology. The timeline in this chapter shows us how their history is our history.

*The universe is
full of magical things,
patiently waiting for our
wits to grow sharper.*

EDEN PHILLPOTTS

HISTORICAL USES OF CRYSTALS

Here's a quick look at how crystals have been used and revered throughout time.

56–40 million years ago

During the Eocene era, ancient trees along the Baltic coast were oozing amber. It's estimated that the ancient forests produced more than 100,000 tons of the stuff.

25,000 years BCE

There's evidence of amulets and talismans being worn during the Upper Palaeolithic era. Made with Baltic amber, these discoveries suggest the gemstone was valued for its beauty as well as protective properties.

c. 14,000–10,500 years BCE

Although much of Native America's history is lost, they revered crystals and used them for healing, ritualizations and as weapons. Crystals were seen as tools from the earth and treated with the utmost respect, only to be used by those who knew how to work with them, such as healers or diviners. The turquoise stone was especially precious and meant "stone of the sky": it was believed to have been created by a combination of rainwater and tears of joy that had sunk into the earth. Many tribes used turquoise in ceremonies and rituals for protection, to bring rain, and even as a currency.

During this time the ancient Sumerians, one of the first civilizations, recorded the use of crystals in healing potions. Incantations and ritualistic practices were performed to ward off evil spirits, and they also used gemstones in their artwork.

Ancient Egyptians favoured lapis lazuli, a deep blue stone, over gold, and used carnelian, turquoise, clear quartz and emerald in their amulets and jewellery for health and protection. It is thought that Cleopatra and other ancient Egyptian royals would wear lapis lazuli in order to access ancient knowledge. Ancient murals and tomb paintings show that malachite was used as eye make-up.

Over this time, four sacred Hindu texts were written. Collectively they were named the "Vedas": Rig-Veda (for recitation), Yajur-Veda (for liturgy), Sama-Veda (for chanting) and Atharva-Veda (magic formulas). The use of crystals to treat certain ailments, as well as their specific properties, are discussed in these texts. Ayurvedic medicine, which is rising in popularity today, is based on these texts.

c. 4500–2000 BCE

c. 3100–330 BCE

c. 1500–1200 BCE

800–600 BCE

In early- to mid-Archaic Greece, crystals were used as talismans, said to protect soldiers in battle. They would rub crushed haematite, a dark, iron-based crystal, on their bodies believing it would make them invincible. Most crystals today still take their names from the Greek language. The word "crystal" itself comes from the Greek *krustallos*, meaning "ice" – the Greeks believed crystals to be permanently frozen water and thought clear quartz was eternal ice gifted from the heavens.

360 BCE

The Greek philosopher Plato (428–348 BCE) wrote one of his most famous texts about the destruction of the ancient civilization of Atlantis, which was said to have existed around 9,000 years before Plato's time. He describes Atlanteans as a highly advanced people who grew too powerful. He writes about their use of crystals in healing and technology, as well as using them to read minds and transmit thoughts. He also mentions advanced healing carried out with large crystal rods.

Ancient Japanese people used crystals for many prophetic and psychic practices. They believed that gazing – or scrying – at crystal would enable you to foresee future events and receive psychic visions. Quartz spheres were known to be representative of the dragon heart, signifying their power and wisdom – it was used to invite greater wisdom and knowledge, not dissimilar to its uses today!

Though Romans enjoyed using crystals in sculptures and jewellery, only wealthier citizens were lucky enough to use them as talismans to provide protection in battle and attract health and good fortune. Jasper, lapis lazuli and onyx were just some of the commonly used stones, while carnelian and garnet were used as amulets. Crystals were also used in medical treatments.

St Epiphanius, Bishop of Salamis in Cyprus, wrote a treatise titled *De Duodecim Lapidibus* (On the Twelve Stones). It speaks about the 12 stones mentioned in the Bible and assigns healing qualities to each one, while also denouncing their supposed magic powers.

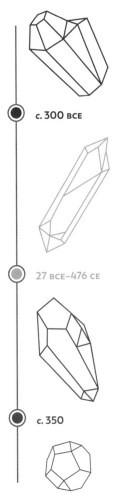

c. **300** BCE

27 BCE–476 CE

c. **350**

355

Amulets were banned by the Christian church, although crystals continued to be popular.

c. 1000

Chinese emperors were buried in jade armour, while jade masks were used in burials at around the same time in Mexico.

c. 1067–81

Marbod, Bishop of Rennes, wrote his *De Lapidibus* (On Gemstones), in which he describes 60 gemstones and their magic properties. He claims that agate would make the wearer more agreeable, persuasive and in favour of God, but he was, naturally, slightly biased.

c. 12th century

Sapphire was the clergy's favourite gem for ecclesiastical rings.

1250

Albertus Magnus, also known as Saint Albert the Great, wrote *De Mineralibus* (On Minerals), a book on minerals within which is a treatise that took a scientific view on stones and their healing properties.

c. 1300

Jade pendants representing the ancestor spirits were worn by the Māoris in New Zealand. The necklaces were passed down from generation to generation through the male line. The belief that green stones are lucky is still prevalent in parts of New Zealand today.

Minerals were highly regarded during the Renaissance period – they were collected and displayed for their external qualities rather than used for their healing properties. The origins of these minerals were a complete mystery; they were unlike plants or animals in that they didn't reproduce, yet the science didn't exist to study them. Royal courts would hire physicians to find new medicines: crushed pearls were mixed into wine and turquoise was worn to treat eyesight.

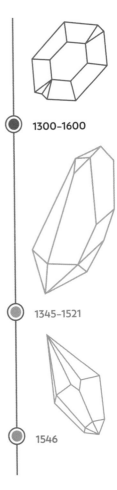

1300–1600

Aztecs honoured their gods by making jewellery from turquoise, jade, opal and amethyst. They developed drills to make holes in the stones as well as methods to grind and polish gemstones. Their jewellery often honoured animals with religious significance, such as snakes and jaguars. Turquoise mosaics, masks and statues were made in honour of Xiuhtecuhtli, the Aztec god of fire (also known as the "Turquoise Lord").

1345–1521

Georg Bauer wrote *De Natura Fossilium*, the first scientific text on minerology, describing the physical characteristics of stones.

1546

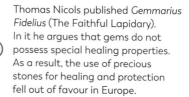

1659

Thomas Nicols published *Gemmarius Fidelius* (The Faithful Lapidary). In it he argues that gems do not possess special healing properties. As a result, the use of precious stones for healing and protection fell out of favour in Europe.

c. 19th century

Advances in science and medicine, as well as investigations into mediums, crystals and faith healers began to increase scepticism around crystal healing as people converted to new medicines. However, in 1880, the Curie brothers discovered piezoelectricity, the process of using crystals to convert mechanical energy into electrical energy, or vice versa.

1970s

Sidelined for some time against growing scepticism, the advent of New Age culture brought a revival of crystals for healing practices. Books started to re-popularize the use of crystals for spiritual well-being. Much of the information was derived from old traditions, experimentation and channelling.

21st century

Crystal therapy is now accepted as a mainstream and complementary therapy, crossing the boundaries of religious and spiritual beliefs.

THE IMPORTANCE OF CRYSTALS TODAY

In a world where we're thinking about the consequences of climate change, the endless whirr of consumerism and never-ending conflict, more people are looking to connect to the natural world. The natural crystalline resources of the earth are being respected again for their benefits to our physical, emotional and spiritual well-being, and they present a more flexible and inclusive approach to self-development and connection with others.

Although crystals are increasingly being used in modern technology they are conversely being recognized for their ability to dissipate the negative side effects of it. As technology grows evermore complicated, the crystals also offer solutions to support and protect us from the unhealthy emanations of our mobiles and laptops.

Crystals have always been there – but the knowledge they contain has sometimes been lost and forgotten. It is comforting to know that in a modern world of stress, overwhelming situations and confusion, there is a crystal available for every conceivable issue, waiting to share its wisdom and positivity.

CRYSTAL CARE 101

Many crystals are fragile and need to be stored correctly, but they may also be holding negative energies from previous use. This chapter will guide you on how to keep your crystals cleansed and charged, so they can work at their best for you.

*The universe buries strange
jewels deep within us all,
and then stands back to
see if we can find them.*

ELIZABETH GILBERT

CLEANSING YOUR CRYSTALS

There are many quick and easy ways to cleanse your crystals. However, not all methods are suitable for every stone, so it's important to know the crystal type and consider its colour and fragility.

Burning sage – also known as smudging – is usually suitable for all crystals. You will need a bunch of dried herbs, such as white sage or scented wood (palo santo is available in any crystal store). Light the herbs with a match or lighter and pass the crystal through the smoke in order to purify it. You can also sage yourself by wafting the herb around your body to clear any negative energies hanging out in your aura. Always take care when using fire and only perform smudging in a ventilated space.

Bathing your crystals in sunlight or moonlight for a few hours is the easiest method of both cleansing and charging. But although all crystals are suitable for cleansing in moonlight, some of them fade in sunlight. The colour rays of the crystal are a big part of its healing make-up, as well as its structure and mineral properties, so faded colour can diminish their healing potential. Some crystals that fade in sunlight are: amethyst, rose quartz, fluorite, turquoise, most calcites, celestite, kunzite and citrine. Generally, lighter colours are more vulnerable to fading.

You can cleanse your crystals by placing them on top of amethyst clusters, clear quartz, carnelian or selenite, but bear in mind that the stones you use to do this will also need regular cleansing themselves.

Hold your crystal under running water, or soak for a few minutes in sea or salt water. Mentally intend for the water to wash all negativity away and for the crystal to recharge itself. Intention is really important when working with crystals, and it means that your thoughts need to be focused and specific so that you can be very clear on what you want the crystal to do. Note: not all crystals are suitable for contact with water, particularly fragile ones such as selenite, kunzite or iron pyrite.

Burying your crystal in the earth is deeply purifying and nurturing (as long as you remember where it is!). If your crystal is particularly fragile, such as kyanite, it can be buried in a small box. Or for a quicker cleanse, put it in a bowl of rice overnight instead.

Sound vibration is excellent for cleansing crystals. You can use tingshas (small Tibetan cymbals, easily available online), singing bowls, a tuning fork, or anything where sound frequency moves energy through the crystal.

You can also blow vigorously on it, as if blowing the negativity away.

A few crystals are said to be exceptions to the rule and are self-cleansing, such as citrine.

CHARGING CRYSTALS

Crystals need to be cleansed first and then recharged with new energy. Often the best way to recharge crystals is with sun, moon or earth energy, although you can also use your intention to help them re-energize.

Cleansing and charging in moonlight

The full moon is the most powerful one in the lunar cycle and the best way to obtain maximum lunar energy for your crystals.

Ideally place your crystals outside on the earth or on your lawn overnight (perhaps on a tray or soft cloth) to charge them with lunar energy, but a windowsill that gets moonlight will also work.

Certain crystals have a particular connection to lunar energy, such as moonstone, selenite, opal and clear quartz, but all crystals are suitable for cleansing and charging in moonlight.

The moon is a water element and said to have a soft feminine or yin energy, representing qualities such as surrender and tranquillity, that are beneficial for mental and emotional health. Different phases of the moon are said to represent different energies, and you may want to investigate and experiment with these.

Cleansing and charging in sunlight

The sun has a glorious warm, happy and go-getting energy that many of us love. Leave your crystals outside in the daylight or on a windowsill for at least 30 minutes and allow them to absorb the sun's rays. Even on a cloudy day, they'll still benefit from this energy, much like humans do.

Crystals that thrive on sun energy are some of the "sunny" looking stones such as sunstone, ruby, carnelian, amber and tiger's eye but a few sunny stones such as orange and yellow calcite and citrine can fade easily, so it's best not to keep them in the sun for long or to use early morning sunlight instead. A few minutes is enough for vulnerable crystals.

The sun is fire energy associated with the masculine, and protects, strengthens, revitalizes and physically heals.

Take care when charging transparent crystals such as clear quartz, as these magnify the sun's rays and could potentially start a fire if resting on a flammable surface.

Cleansing and charging in the earth

Bury your crystal in the earth for a few days, but remember to mark the spot!

PROGRAMMING A CRYSTAL

Programming a crystal means you set an intention on how you'd like it to work for you. Crystals retain their programming (unless you change it and ask them to assist you in a different way) so when you reconnect with it, it will continue to work with you in the way you asked it to.

Here are some easy steps for programming a crystal:

- Find somewhere quiet and take a few deep breaths to relax, while holding your crystal. Close your eyes.

- Try and "tune in" to your crystal – this means thinking about its colour, shape and texture and feeling its energies.

- Now set your intention with the crystal and instruct it on how you would like it to work with you. If you like, you can write this down on a piece of paper. For example: "I would like this amethyst to assist me with peaceful sleep." Be as clear as you can.

- Visualize the crystal assisting you in the way you've asked, place the crystal on your heart, and thank it.

Even after a crystal is programmed, it can still bring to the surface anything else that needs healing; you can also programme a crystal with multiple intentions to help you in a variety of ways.

Why should you programme your crystals?

Programming a crystal focuses its energies on a goal, intention or desire and allows it to work effectively with purpose, so it's important to be as clear and specific as possible. It also minimizes the chance of the crystal acting on a wrong thought or intention. Your crystal can be an even bigger cheerleader if it knows exactly how you wish it to help you, and it's a great way to start building a bond with your crystal.

In the Renaissance period, gemstones were thought to have been corrupted by the original sins of Adam and potentially inhabited by demons. Crystals could also be tainted if they were handled by a sinner. Therefore, Renaissance belief dictated that they should be sanctified and consecrated before wearing. This belief is still in evidence today in the cleansing and programming of crystals before use.

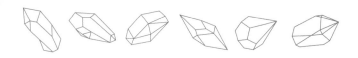

STORING YOUR CRYSTALS

Fragility and colour are the two main things you should consider when deciding how to store your crystals. Crystals are fragile, and as some are softer than others they are more prone to scratching. Care should be taken in storing them.

When your crystals aren't in use they can be wrapped in something soft, such as a cloth. This prevents them from scratching each other and protects them from picking up negative energies.

THE MOHS SCALE

It's useful to know where each of your crystals sits on the Mohs scale (these values are provided in the crystal profiles in this book). The scale rates a mineral's hardness from 1 to 10, with 1 being the most fragile, and 10 the hardest. Talc is at number 1 as the softest mineral, while diamond, at a rating of 10, is one of the hardest minerals known to man, with the most resistance to scratching.

Once you know how hard or soft your crystal is, you will be able to discern how prone it is to scratching, or even dissolving. Selenite, for example, only has a Mohs scale rating of 2, and dissolves in water.

Lighter-coloured crystals are more prone to fading from direct sunlight and may need to be kept somewhere shady or dark, while darker-coloured crystals could happily be kept in a display case.

When they aren't being used, all crystals should be stored apart except for tumbled stones (small polished stones which are readily available in gem shops), which are more robust and can be kept together. There are special specimen-style cases (similar to display cases in museums) that you can make use of. However, an old box and some padding material, such as soft cloth, can also be used.

ADDITIONAL CARE TIPS

Most crystals are safe to handle, but there are a few stones that contain potentially toxic minerals and require some simple care by the user. This usually involves washing your hands after handling them. The most common of these stones are: malachite (use only in polished form), galena, mohawkite, wulfenite, cinnabar and cerussite. These stones should come with a warning when buying them but if you're unsure, there is plenty of information on the internet regarding individual stones.

CRYSTALS FOR SELF-CARE

Self-care is often overlooked as we navigate our way through busy lives, but it's a crucial part of keeping ourselves healthy: physically, mentally, emotionally and spiritually. Meditating with the soothing crystals in the next chapter will help you feel like a serene god or goddess, ready to tackle the day ahead!

Genius is the ability to receive from the universe.

I CHING

ROSE QUARTZ

The number one stone for self-care, the gentle rose quartz is the stone of unconditional love – that includes for ourselves. It reveals the true essence of love, opening the heart at all levels and healing heartache. For those who are single, this stone can attract love and relationships; for those in a couple, this stone promotes unconditional love and restores trust and harmony.

This peaceful stone soothes and reassures, especially in situations of trauma, crisis or grief. It supports self-forgiveness, inviting you to trust and value yourself. The rose quartz is a good stone to rely on during a mid-life crisis, as it helps with accepting necessary change.

Place in the relationship corner of a room – this can be found in the far right-hand corner (looking inwards to the room from the door).

- **Appearance:** Pink, all sizes. Generally translucent.
- **Mohs scale hardness:** 7
- **Associated chakras:** Heart
- **Care instructions:** Fades in direct sunlight.
- **Additional tips for use:** Wear or place over the heart. Place on the thymus (between the lungs) to help with chest problems.

MOONSTONE

You guessed it – moonstone is connected to moon energy and intuition. It's excellent for female issues, such as the reproductive cycle, menstrual-related issues and hormones. This nurturing stone calms emotions, overreactions and emotional triggers. Like the moon over water, it's reflective; it reminds us that everything is cyclic and in flux, and that change is inevitable.

A stone of new beginnings, it asks you to be open to serendipity. But take care you don't get carried away – moonstone can result in illusions if you've been doing too much wishful thinking. Lucid dreaming can be enjoyed with this stone, especially at full moon, and you may find your psychic abilities increasing.

- **Appearance:** White, cream, yellow, green-blue. All sizes. Often pearlescent, milky, translucent.
- **Mohs scale hardness:** 6–6.5
- **Associated chakras:** Crown, third eye
- **Additional tips for use:** Place on third eye for spiritual journeying; solar plexus or heart to soothe or dissolve negative emotional patterns. Some women may need to take it easy with the moonstone at full moon!
- **Fun fact:** Some ancient cultures believed the stone was created from moonbeams.

IRON PYRITE

Also known as Fool's Gold, this glittering treasure is anything but foolish. From the Greek *pyr*, meaning "fire", it emits sparks when struck onto steel. Its positive, sunny energy boosts self-esteem and blasts away feelings of inadequacy. Stimulating pyrite wants to fill you with ideas and help you tap into your abilities and full potential. It's also a great shield against pollutants and negative energy, and teaches you that "all that glitters is not gold". In other words, it helps you to see the truth behind the façade.

A great anxiety reliever, it can help you to emerge from fatigue, melancholy and deep despair and its vibrant rays increase mood and energy.

- **Appearance:** Gold to brown, small to medium. Metallic-looking, sometimes cubic.
- **Mohs scale hardness:** 6–6.5
- **Associated chakras:** Solar plexus
- **Care instructions:** Not suitable for contact with water.
- **Fun fact:** The Kaurna people of South Australia use flintstone, stringy bark tinder and pyrite as a traditional method of starting a fire.

BLUE LACE AGATE

This lacy-patterned gem is a wonderful healer, known to be particularly powerful for the throat. Its waves of soft, soothing energy give it a deserved reputation as one of the great nurturing and supportive stones.

Blue lace agate resolves suppressed feelings that stem from a fear of being judged and rejected, with a specific focus on judgement in the parent-child relationship. It helps to aid free expression of thoughts and feelings that may have felt previously blocked from childhood.

This calming gem is said to soothe and neutralize anger, infection, inflammation and fever, and brings deep peace from the highest vibrations. As it activates, clears and heals the throat chakra, you may find that higher spiritual truths can be expressed.

- **Appearance:** Pale blue, banded with white or dark blue lines. Usually small, tumbled.
- **Mohs scale hardness:** 6.5–7
- **Associated chakras:** Throat
- **Additional tips for use:** Effective for sound healing – use to focus and direct sound to a specific area. Wear as a pendant on or near the throat chakra.

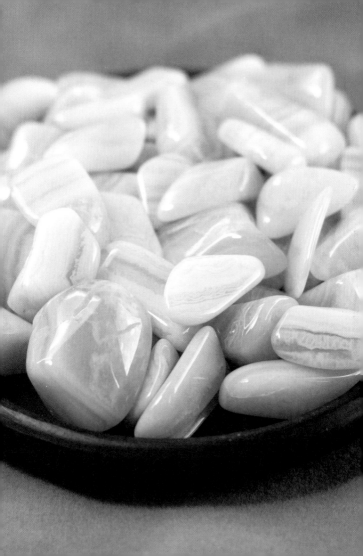

SUNSTONE

Like its name suggests, this sunny, joyful stone will remind you of the sweetness of life when you're feeling low. It encourages self-nurturance and dissipates feelings of failure, promoting healthy self-esteem. To this end, it removes co-dependent tendencies, does away with procrastination and removes the draining "hooks" other people might have attached to you. Carry sunstone with you if you struggle to say no to others.

Traditionally linked to good luck and fortune, meditate with sunstone to experience profound connection to the light and sun energy in everyday life. The light and energy this little stone will bring allows your true self to shine.

- **Appearance:** Yellow, orange, red-brown. Often small and tumbled. Can be clear or opaque, shimmering.
- **Mohs scale hardness:** 6–7
- **Associated chakras:** Solar plexus, sacral
- **Additional tips for use:** Loves to be charged and meditated with in the sun. Draws out and dissolves repressed emotions when placed on solar plexus.
- **Fun fact:** In Native American lore, when a great warrior was injured by an arrow, his blood fell onto some Oregon sunstone. His warrior spirit seeped into the stones, colouring them red and giving them sacred power.

CRYSTALS FOR HEALING

All crystals have healing benefits, but the five crystals detailed in this chapter are master healers on multiple levels, and their potency can help to repair and enrich many areas of your life.

Have dominion over your awareness and you'll have dominion over your destiny.

MICHAEL BECKWITH

CLEAR QUARTZ

Known as the master healer, clear quartz is a powerful energy amplifier and healer. Because it contains every colour, it works on all levels and can offer healing for every disorder.

Clear quartz is also a master at focusing thought and unlocking memory; it is excellent for concentration and allows you to see and think clearly. It regulates energy by absorbing, storing or releasing it, and draws off any negativity, including neutralizing background radiation and electromagnetic smog.

Quartz is one of the most commonly found minerals on Earth, and because it's piezoelectrical it can conduct electric currents, making it very useful in technology as well as healing.

- **Appearance:** Clear. Usually in points or clusters. All sizes.
- **Mohs scale hardness:** 7
- **Associated chakras:** All
- **Care instructions:** Clear quartz can magnify the sun's rays – don't leave it on a flammable surface.
- **Fun fact:** Keeping your watch on, even at night, helps it to keep time better – the quartz crystal inside performs better when kept at an even temperature.

MALACHITE

This psychedelic-looking stone is predicted to be one of the most important of the future, as it's said to be helping to heal the Earth by grounding spiritual energies. Its elaborate patterning can conjure images and dreams and facilitate access to other worlds. Known as a stone of transformation, it can shake things up and encourage adventure. It can bring patterns inhibiting your growth to the surface, while opening the heart to unconditional love.

Malachite absorbs negative energies and pollutants easily.

- **Appearance:** Green, banded. All sizes, usually tumbled or polished.

- **Mohs scale hardness:** 7

- **Associated chakras:** Heart, third eye

- **Care instructions:** Cleanse on a quartz cluster in sunlight before and after use. Malachite can be damaged by salt. Absorb negative emotions by placing on the solar plexus. Can cause mild heart palpitations – if this happens, replace with rose quartz or rhodonite.

- **Fun fact:** Malachite got its name from the Greek word for mallow, "*moloche*", due to a similarity between the ripple-patterned stone and mallow leaves.

AMBER

This fire-coloured gem is actually fossilized pine tree resin with a strong connection to the earth. A powerful healer and cleanser, it is believed to bring disease to the surface for clearance and promote tissue revitalization, helping the body to heal.

An environment and chakra cleanser, it turns negative energies into positive ones, and its warm, sunny energy helps achieve a positive mental state. It absorbs pain and negative energy, flooding the body with vitality and is a wonderful stress reliever and protector. Amber brings stability and stimulates the intellect and creative self-expression. This wise stone also helps the wearer to trust.

- **Appearance:** Orange, golden brown, yellow. Various sizes. Opaque or clear; may have flora or insects trapped inside.
- **Mohs scale hardness:** 2–2.5
- **Associated chakras:** Sacral, solar plexus
- **Care instructions:** Scratches easily; burns at high temperatures. Perfume and soaking in water can damage the surface.
- **Fun fact:** If you want to check your amber for authenticity, the real thing floats as it's so light.

FLUORITE

Fluorite is highly stabilizing, and the best crystal for overcoming disorganization and chaos. This is a stone of progress, and will organize and structure your life for you! A powerful healer, it specializes in infections and disorders, and its organizing abilities help to restore perfect order to the body and mind, meaning it's useful for mental disorders. Excellent for clearing stress and negative energies, this purifying stone can speed up your spiritual awakening by linking it to the universal mind.

Cleansing fluorite helps you to see past illusions to the truth, so you can let go of fixed patterns and see the bigger picture.

- **Appearance:** Clear, green, yellow, brown, purple, blue. All sizes. Transparent.
- **Mohs scale hardness:** 4
- **Associated chakras:** All, depending on colour
- **Care instructions:** Fluorite needs cleansing after each use as it's so effective at absorbing negative vibes and stress.
- **Additional tips for use:** Stroke across body toward heart to alleviate pain. Excellent placed in your environment or used as a palm stone.

RHODONITE

This very special stone is a master emotional healer and is named from the Greek *rhodon*, meaning "rose", after its lovely pink colour. Often called the relationship stone, it awakens and clears the heart and nurtures unconditional love, both of the self and others.

It teaches compassion and forgiveness in order to heal long-term abuse and trauma.

Rhodonite is especially good for those who have a tendency toward self-destruction, or abusive or co-dependent relationships. It brings resentment or anger to the surface for clearance and encourages clear communication, helping you identify what you're projecting on to others. It promotes calm in dangerous or distressing situations.

- **Appearance:** Pink or red, usually small and tumbled. Marbled, with black veins.
- **Mohs scale hardness:** 7
- **Associated chakras:** Heart
- **Additional tips for use:** Rhodonite heals emotional and physical wounds. Place over the heart, or on the skin for external/internal wounds.
- **Fun fact:** Rhodonite has been the national stone of Russia since 1913. There, it is known as "the eagle stone", as eagles like to take pieces of it to line their nests!

CRYSTALS FOR PROSPERITY

Who wouldn't enjoy a little prosperity in their life? The crystals in the next chapter are some of the most beneficial stones to work with for success in a business venture or simply to open your eyes to the many riches (not just financial) that life has to offer. Here's to success!

*If you want to find the
secrets of the universe,
think in terms of energy,
frequency and vibration.*

NIKOLA TESLA

CITRINE

This cheerful yellow stone of abundance attracts wealth and prosperity. It takes its name from the French *citron*, meaning "lemon", and brings sunshine and success to all areas of life. Its warming, energizing vibe promotes joy and creativity, clearing negative energies from your home and creating emotional balance in your own energy field. This generous stone also enhances self-esteem, helping you to create a positive outlook on life.

Place citrine in the wealth corner of your home or business: the area farthest back and left (looking inwards) from your front door.

Citrine can also be useful in tackling depression, fears and phobias, menstrual and menopausal issues and Chronic Fatigue Syndrome.

- **Appearance:** Yellow, yellow-brown, smoky-grey brown. Transparent. All sizes, found as a geode, point or cluster. Natural citrine is usually a pale yellow colour, but most citrine on the market is heat-treated quartz and is a darker yellow-brown.
- **Mohs scale hardness:** 7
- **Associated chakras:** Solar plexus, sacral, crown
- **Care instructions:** Fades in sunlight.
- **Additional tips for use:** Place citrine on your solar plexus during meditation to improve confidence.

AVENTURINE

This special glittering stone has its own adjective, *aventurescence*, to describe its sparkly appearance. Made up of reflective mineral particles, it is known as a prosperous stone that promotes leadership qualities and decision-making. Also an excellent stone for compassion and perseverance, it helps to neutralize negative situations and dissipates anger and irritation. Its stabilizing energies enhance creativity and protect against environmental pollution.

The most common form of the stone is green aventurine. Known as the heart healer, its soothing colour facilitates well-being and emotional calm. It guards the heart against psychic vampirism, assists it to heal, and facilitates harmony between the mind and heart. Green aventurine teaches us to trust our intuition, connect with our inner joy and synchronize ourselves with nature.

- **Appearance:** Green, red, peach, blue, brown. All sizes. Opaque, flecked with glittery bits.
- **Mohs scale hardness:** 6–7
- **Associated chakras:** Heart
- **Care instructions:** Fades in sunlight.
- **Fun fact:** In ancient Chinese culture, aventurine was the sacred stone of Kuan-Yin, the goddess of mercy.

MOSS AGATE

This optimistic stone is known to attract wealth and abundance and encourages trust and hope. Its beautiful mossy tones symbolize a strong connection with nature, encouraging growth and inspiration again after a period of stagnation. The stabilizing energy of this stone can provide insight into depression brought about through life circumstances. Supporting new beginnings and personal transformation, it can refresh the soul and assist the wearer in seeing beauty in the world.

Moss agate works to improve self-esteem by strengthening positive personality traits and releasing deep-rooted fears and stress. Helpful against environmental pollutants, it's believed to be an anti-inflammatory, and can help with recuperation and neutralizing long-term illness.

- **Appearance:** Green, yellow, red, blue, brown. Small, tumbled, "woodland" patterns like moss or lichen, transparent or translucent.
- **Mohs scale hardness:** 6.5–7
- **Associated chakras:** Heart
- **Fun fact:** Moss agate is not an agate. It's a type of chalcedony, a mineral of the quartz family. It was named before it was scientifically described and the name stuck. Also, the stone is usually formed from weathered volcanic rocks and doesn't contain organic matter.

CARNELIAN

The carnelian is a fascinating and dynamic stone that appears to have contradictory powers, yet balances them perfectly. Placing one near the front door protects the home while also attracting abundance, and it works intensely to ground your energy while restoring vitality and motivation.

Sharpening concentration, the carnelian focuses daydreamers during meditation but can soothe anger and protect against envy and resentment, whether it's yours or somebody else's.

It stimulates metabolism and is useful for overcoming abuse, helping you to trust yourself and your intuition. Its ability to inspire creativity makes it an ideal crystal for creatives, and it promotes courage and success.

- **Appearance:** Red, orange, pink, brown. Often small and tumbled. Translucent.

- **Mohs scale hardness:** 7

- **Associated chakras:** Root, sacral

- **Additional tips for use:** Carnelian can be used to cleanse other stones (but remember to keep your carnelian regularly cleansed too).

- **Fun fact:** The carnelian was nicknamed the "setting sun" by the ancient Egyptians and has associations with solar and fire energies.

JADE

Traditionally known as a good luck stone, jade is particularly valued in Eastern cultures and is thought to promote the flow of prosperity and abundance.

To improve the feng shui of your home, place a jade stone or ornament near the front door to invite in wealth and good luck. A three-legged frog or a fish carved from jade are said to be especially fortuitous – if you put a coin into the mouth of these willing ornamental creatures your wealth will multiply!

Jade is also associated with wisdom and harmony and stimulates the heart chakra, encouraging love, nurturance and self-healing. Excellent for calming the mind and facilitating emotional release, it's helpful in easing irritability!

- **Appearance:** Green, blue-green, blue, cream, white, lavender, orange, red, brown. All sizes. Jade made from jadeite is translucent, jade formed from nephrite is creamy.

- **Mohs scale hardness:** 6.5–7

- **Associated chakras:** Heart

- **Additional tips for use:** Jade's silky and cool exterior makes it an excellent "worry" stone, as it soothes the emotions when stroked or touched.

- **Fun fact:** During the Stone Age, jade was used to make axe heads, knives and other weapons because its smooth texture is good for intricate carvings.

CRYSTALS
FOR
MEDITATION

Find it hard to meditate? The crystals in the next chapter will come to your aid. Meditating with one of these soothing stones will help you to feel calm and connect you with the higher realms.

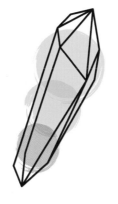

*Follow your
inner moonlight.*

ALLEN GINSBERG

KUNZITE

Named after the vice president of Tiffany & Co. and mineralogist George Frederick Kunz, this delightful crystal awakens the heart to unconditional love. Its high vibrations allow a deep meditative state to be reached easily.

Radiating peace, its tranquil rays protect the wearer from unwanted negative energies and assist the body to recover from emotional stress. Kunzite contains lithium, a natural mood enhancer, meaning this stone is good for relieving depression and anxiety.

- **Appearance:** Pink, lilac, green, clear, yellow. All sizes. Transparent or translucent, striated (bladed).
- **Mohs scale hardness:** 6.5–7
- **Associated chakras:** Crown
- **Care instructions:** Brittle, susceptible to fracture in sudden or high heat, fades in sunlight.
- **Fun fact:** In 1963, President John F. Kennedy bought his wife Jackie a 47-carat kunzite ring for Christmas. Assassinated in November of that year, he never got the chance to give it to her. After Jackie's death, the ring fetched over $415,000 at auction.

KYANITE

Named from the Greek word *kyanos*, or "blue", this calming stone is often the colour of the sky. Its tranquillizing rays stimulate psychic abilities, opening the higher mind and facilitating connection with spirit guides and spiritual truth. Its stabilizing energy replenishes the physical body.

It assists with opening the throat chakra, strengthening the ability to speak your truth, easing confusion, fear, anger, frustration and stress. Blue kyanite is particularly useful for the throat and voice and is a good stone for performers or public speakers.

The pearly wisdom of the kyanite teaches the part played by the individual in their own life, and removes reliance on the ideas of blind fate or karma.

- **Appearance:** Blue-white, black, grey, green. All sizes. Striated (bladed), pearly lustre, transparent or opaque.
- **Mohs scale hardness:** 4.5–7 depending on cut
- **Associated chakras:** Throat
- **Care instructions:** Kyanite is fragile and breaks easily.
- **Fun fact:** Kyanite has two types of hardness. Lengthways, it grades 4 to 5 on the Mohs scale, but widthways it grades 6 to 7. This makes it a tricky beast to cut.

PREHNITE

This crystal of unconditional love induces deep meditation, allowing you to access information from your higher mind. Meditating with prehnite is said to plug you in to the universe's energy grid, where you may encounter angels and other spiritual beings. Sometimes called the "prophecy stone", prehnite can be used for divination, and enables you to be prepared for any situation. It helps to restore your faith in the universe and can illuminate the way for your spiritual growth.

It eases nightmares, phobias and deep-seated fears, and teaches you to be in harmony with nature and the universe.

- **Appearance:** Green, yellow, brown, white. Small to medium; translucent.
- **Mohs scale hardness:** 6–6.5
- **Associated chakras:** Heart, third eye
- **Additional tips for use:** Place on the third eye for prophecy.
- **Fun fact:** The Chinese call it grape jade – when raw, its typical bubbly formation resembles a bunch of grapes!

SELENITE

Named after the ancient Greek goddess of the moon, this heavenly stone is most commonly pure white. The high vibration of selenite helps clear confusion, aiding clarity and insight and completely calming the mind and aura. It also helps the user to access angelic consciousness and the higher realms. The deep peace and divine connection that selenite brings can be particularly useful for meditation or spiritual work. It can be useful for accessing your life plan, showing you the lessons that you're still working on and how you can progress through them.

- **Appearance:** Mostly white; can also be orange, brown, blue, green. Translucent, ribbed. All sizes.
- **Mohs scale hardness:** 2
- **Associated chakras:** Crown
- **Care instructions:** Selenite is extremely fragile and dissolves in water.
- **Fun fact:** In ancient times, selenite was believed to banish evil spirits, and is said to inhabit the place between light and matter.

SMOKY QUARTZ

This smoky gem is one of the best stones for grounding, stress relief and relaxation. During meditation, it helps the brain to move between alpha and beta states, keeping the mind calm and clear and raising your vibration.

The protective smoky quartz fortifies the nerves, relieving fear, suicidal tendencies and depression, leaving a feeling of tranquillity. A detoxifier, it blocks geopathic and electromagnetic stress and clears negative vibrations.

- **Appearance:** Smoky brown/black or yellowish tinge towards the end of a clear quartz. All sizes. Translucent. Artificially heated smoky quartz will look very black and opaque.
- **Mohs scale hardness:** 7
- **Associated chakras:** Root, earth star
- **Additional tips for use:** For stress relief, sit with a stone in each hand. Smoky quartz can relieve pain when placed on the painful area. Position points away from the body to draw off negative energies, and toward the body to energize.
- **Fun fact:** In 12th-century China, layers of smoky quartz were worn over the eyes to protect them from the sun – an early example of sunglasses.

CRYSTALS FOR STRESS

There's no doubt that modern life is stressful. There seems so much to do and so little time to do it. Take some time out with some of the crystals in the next chapter, and melt away the stresses and strains of the day.

*Crystals amplify
the consciousness.*

SHIRLEY MacLAINE

JASPER

Known as a supreme nurturer, jasper comes in many different shades and patterns. It is highly supportive during stressful times, replacing anxiety with tranquillity. It will also ground you when you feel that everything's whirling crazily around you, and is believed to absorb any type of negative energy, including environmental and electromagnetic pollution.

This wonderful stone is a useful support during periods of prolonged illness or hospitalization and helps to re-energize the body. Red jasper in particular makes an excellent worry bead or palm stone.

- **Appearance:** Red, brown, yellow, green, blue, purple. Opaque, sometimes patterned. Tumbled or raw.

- **Mohs scale hardness:** 6.5–7

- **Associated chakras:** All

- **Additional tips for use:** Jasper works slowly – use for long periods of time. A large piece of brown jasper will absorb the negative energy in a room.

- **Fun fact:** Jasper was once thought to ward off evil spirits, and even protect against snake and spider bites. In the 4th century, jasper was used to encourage rain.

CALCITE

Calcite is a great emotional stress reliever and brings peace of mind. It's a strong cleanser, environmentally and within the body, where it eliminates stagnant energy.

It can provide positivity when lacking in hope or motivation, calming the mind and aiding discernment and insight. It is said to convert ideas into action and be useful for study. It hastens spiritual growth, facilitating connection to higher realms while stabilizing and encouraging trust in oneself. Calcite is also useful in helping you to conquer setbacks.

Blue calcite in particular is great for recuperating and soothing stress. Mangano calcite relieves anxiety and is ideal for anyone who has suffered trauma or assault.

- **Appearance:** Blue, green, orange, yellow, clear, brown, pink (mangano), red. All sizes, sometimes banded. Tumbled or raw. Waxy, translucent.

- **Mohs scale hardness:** 3

- **Associated chakras:** All, depending on colour

- **Care instructions:** Easily scratched. Light-coloured calcites such as blue or green fade in sunlight.

- **Fun fact:** Calcite has more uses than nearly any other mineral and is the main component of limestone and marble. It's used to neutralize acid in fields and rivers, as well as our bellies. It can be found in antacid tablets (as calcium carbonate) and in whitening agent for paint.

CELESTITE

Celestite helps to maintain a harmonious atmosphere during stressful periods. The deep peace it brings can be helpful in resolving conflict, holding the space for peaceful negotiation. Soothing fiery emotions and mental distress, it eases physical tension and helps to dissolve your worries.

Celestite contains divine energies and facilitates contact with the angelic realms. Excellent for enlightenment and spiritual growth, it can enhance your clairvoyant tendencies! A stone of good fortune, celestite teaches the heart to be pure and reveals truth. It reminds you to trust in the divine, dissolving pain and bringing in love.

Most commonly found as a beautiful sky-blue cluster, this crystal will have a balancing effect on your life and promote peaceful coexistence.

- **Appearance:** Blue, white, yellow, red. Medium to large geodes or clusters; transparent.
- **Mohs scale hardness:** 3–3.5
- **Associated chakras:** Throat
- **Care instructions:** Fragile – treat with care and keep out of direct sunlight.
- **Additional tips for use:** Placing a celestite in the room raises its vibrations.

LAPIS LAZULI

Prized by the ancient Egyptians, this beautiful crystal derives its name from the Latin word for stone, "*lapis*", and the Arabic *lazaward*, which denotes its sky-blue pigment. It's great for releasing stress and bringing deep peace. It can ease pain, especially migraines.

This stone also opens the third eye, encouraging spiritual journeying and dreams, and assisting the wearer in the development of their psychic abilities. Protective, it prevents psychic attack.

It balances the throat chakra and reveals inner truth, so be ready and willing to increase your self-awareness! It also releases repressed anger from the throat and aids self-expression. Lapis can be used for assistance with insomnia, and is known to inspire creativity.

- **Appearance:** Deep blue, with gold or white inflections. All sizes, often tumbled.
- **Mohs scale hardness:** 5
- **Associated chakras:** Third eye, throat
- **Fun fact:** Michelangelo used lapis lazuli powder to get the striking blue visible in his frescoes at the Sistine Chapel.

LEPIDOLITE

From the Greek word *lepidos*, meaning "scale", lepidolite is formed of tiny layers. This is a stress-busting stone, useful for anything from computer stress and sick building syndrome to soothing sleep disturbances and emotional stress. This is a calming stone that brings deep emotional healing. It dissolves negativity so is good for depression, and it contains lithium, helpful in stabilizing mood swings and bipolar disorders.

It removes blockages from past lives and can stop obsessive thoughts, helping with addictions and emotional or mental dependencies. Known as a stone of transition, it releases old patterns. Excellent for menopause, it also encourages holding your own space, away from the influence of others.

- **Appearance:** Purple, pink. All sizes. Can be in thin shiny layers (raw), or look grainy (polished).
- **Mohs scale hardness:** 2.5–3
- **Associated chakras:** Throat, heart, third eye and crown
- **Care instructions:** Soft stone vulnerable to flaking. Do not cleanse with water.
- **Fun fact:** When placed over disease on the body, lepidolite gently vibrates.

CRYSTALS FOR SLEEP

That all-important shut-eye can prove elusive after a hectic day and it can be hard to wind down. Light some candles and enjoy a relaxing bath before putting one of these suggested crystals under your pillow for a restful night's sleep. Sweet dreams!

*True manifesting is
allowing the universe to
catch up with your dreams.*

GABRIELLE BERNSTEIN

HAEMATITE

With a name derived from the Greek word for blood, "*haema*", haematite is full of strengthening iron and is a wonderful grounding and protecting stone. Harmonizing the mind, body and spirit, it dissolves negativity and stops unhelpful energies penetrating the aura, allowing the body to feel centred and secure. This ability to bring everything into a state of balance means it can eliminate insomnia caused by a scattered mind.

The strong energy of this stone is also hugely beneficial in boosting confidence, especially in women, and helps you to frame mistakes as learning experiences. It goes without saying that this is an excellent stone for any blood-related issues.

- **Appearance:** Silver-grey, black, red.
  All sizes, polished or raw, heavy.
- **Mohs scale hardness:** 6.5–7
- **Associated chakras:** Root
- **Care instructions:** Haematite should
  not be used for long periods of time, or
  directly where inflammation is present.
- **Fun fact:** Haematite is the world's main source
  of iron ore and is used in science and medicine
  to protect equipment against radiation.

CHAROITE

Charoite takes its name from the Chara River in Siberia, close to the Murun Mountains, the only place where it's currently found. This vibrant purple stone is known to overcome insomnia by inducing deep sleep with vivid dreams.

Aiding transformation and spiritual insight, charoite releases deep fears and helps to put things in perspective. It asks you to accept the present moment as perfect while raising your vibration. This crystal has a relaxing energy that facilitates acceptance of others and reduces worry. It re-energizes the body when exhausted and supports deep physical and emotional healing.

- **Appearance:** Purple. Small to medium, veined or with swirly or mottled patterns. Opaque.
- **Mohs scale hardness:** 5–6
- **Associated chakras:** Heart, third eye, crown
- **Fun fact:** Charoite's spirally strands can make it look a bit psychedelic. This can mean that it's often mistaken for a man-made stone.

HOWLITE

This cool dude is a wonderful remedy for insomnia – incredibly calming and easily placed under a pillow to slow down whirling thoughts. Its ability to still the mind is excellent for meditation.

Need help in achieving your ambitions? Howlite's chilled-out vibe allows for balanced and reasoned communication while strengthening positive character traits. It also supports memory, preaches patience and alleviates uncontrolled anger. Keep it in your pocket to absorb negative energy. Howlite relieves emotional turmoil, especially if it's connected to a past-life cause. Placing it on the third eye can give you insight into other lifetimes and help with any necessary resolution.

- **Appearance:** White with small grey, brown or black veins. All sizes. Marbled, tumbled. Often artificially dyed green or blue to resemble turquoise, or red to resemble coral.
- **Mohs scale hardness:** 3.5
- **Associated chakras:** Third eye
- **Fun fact:** Howlite has been called the "snow leopard stone" for its resemblance to the fur of these gorgeous big cats. Perhaps they're also big on howling?

CHRYSOPRASE

Originating from the ancient Greek words *chrys* – "gold" – and *prasino* – "green" – this beautiful stone is said to promote truth and hope. Able to induce deep meditative states, its calming vibes are perfect for relaxation and peaceful sleep. It's especially effective for children and can reduce nightmares. In adults, it helps to heal the inner child by releasing emotions still stuck in childhood.

It's also said to promote forgiveness and compassion, facilitating both acceptance of the self and others, and is useful in romance and relationships through its connection to the heart chakra. It also works to energize the sacral chakra, encouraging creativity and the full use of one's talents. A strong detoxifier, chrysoprase is believed to stimulate liver function and can help to eliminate heavy metals from the body.

- **Appearance:** Light (apple) green to deep green, lemon. Small, tumbled or raw. Opaque, with flecks.
- **Mohs scale hardness:** 6–7
- **Associated chakras:** Heart, sacral
- **Care instructions:** Sunlight and heat can fade chrysoprase's stunning colour.
- **Fun fact:** Chrysoprase adorns many buildings in Prague, the most famous of which is the Chapel of St Wenceslas.

SODALITE

Named after its high sodium content, this vivacious blue stone is brilliant for tidying the mind, making it an ideal stone to soothe insomnia. It clears mental confusion and calms the brain. Meditating with this stone stimulates the third eye and allows information to flow from the higher mind. Emotionally balancing, sodalite can ease panic attacks.

It releases old conditioning and brings shadow qualities to the surface for acceptance without judgement – sodalite stone will cut to the chase! As it drives toward the truth, it can help defensive or oversensitive personalities release their core fears.

Working to enhance self-esteem and self-trust, at a physical level this stone combats radiation damage and electromagnetic pollution.

- **Appearance:** Blue, either dark or a light blue-white. All sizes.
- **Mohs scale hardness:** 5.5–6
- **Associated chakras:** Throat, third eye
- **Fun fact:** In 1901, the future King George V and Queen Mary had 130 tons of sodalite shipped from Canada to the UK. It was allegedly used to decorate their home, Marlborough House.

CRYSTALS FOR LIFE

The crystals in the next chapter are great for strength and support in this game we call Life. Whether everything's rosy or you're going through tough times, these all-rounders will have something for you.

*Ride the energy of your
own unique spirit.*

GABRIELLE ROTH

BLACK TOURMALINE

There are many different colours of tourmaline, each with their own specific healing abilities, but the black tourmaline is an excellent stone to have around. Deeply protective, it will keep negative energies away, and can be worn as a pendant or placed by your front door.

Black tourmaline, sometimes known as schorl, is very grounding. It is thought to dissolve tension and stress, and fills the gap that negative energies once occupied with life-force energy and vitality. It assists clear and objective thought processes, and encourages you to have a positive attitude, no matter what.

It is said to defend against debilitating disease and strengthen the immune system. It can also prove useful for dyslexia, arthritis and pain relief.

Black tourmaline points draw off negative energy from the body and aura when pointed outwards.

- **Appearance:** Black, striated, sometimes shiny and opaque. All sizes.
- **Mohs scale hardness:** 7–7.5
- **Associated chakras:** Root
- **Care instructions:** Susceptible to flaking.
- **Additional tips for use:** Black tourmaline protects against electromagnetic smog and radiation, so it's helpful to have a piece near electronic goods to absorb their emanations.

TURQUOISE

Worn as a protective amulet for millennia, this lovely pale blue stone is said to provide solace for the spirit and well-being for the body. A natural purifier and mood-stabilizer, turquoise disperses negative energy and infuses inner calm. This gem is your bridge between the physical and spiritual, uniting the Earth and Sky and combining male and female energies.

A strengthening stone that supports self-realization and blows up self-sabotage, it's also capable of inspiring romantic love. Excellent for exhaustion, depression and panic attacks, turquoise is the only gem to have had a colour named after it.

- **Appearance:** Turquoise, green or blue. All sizes. Opaque, sometimes veined. Often polished.
- **Mohs scale hardness:** 5–6
- **Associated chakras:** Throat
- **Care instructions:** Direct sunlight, cosmetics and excessive heat can cause turquoise to fade.
- **Fun fact:** Known as the "sky stone" by the inhabitants of the Himalayas, children in Tibet are gifted a turquoise to protect them on their life journey.

SHUNGITE

Renowned for its ability to absorb geopathic and electromagnetic pollution, shungite is the go-to stone for shielding against nasties. It absorbs anything toxic to health, from pesticides to microwaves. As well as clearing the physical body, it also clears mental and emotional pollutants. Said to have a powerful effect on the immune system, it restores emotional balance and dissipates stress.

Found mainly in Karelia, northern Russia, shungite has been classified as at least two billion years old. This amazing stone contains almost all of the minerals in the periodic table and its potential is still being investigated.

- **Appearance:** Black, any size. Light, due to its carbon composition.
- **Mohs scale hardness:** 3.5–4
- **Care instructions:** Cleanse regularly and place in sunlight to recharge. Shungite is fairly fragile and easily damaged.
- **Additional tips for use:** Wear shungite or tape discs to the back of your phone, computer, TV and other electrical equipment.
- **Fun fact:** Shungite is found in Lake Onega. The highly polluted lake is purified by the shungite bed, and used as a healing spa.

TIGER'S EYE

This eye-catching tiger-striped stone combines earth and sun energy, which results in a very grounding yet high-vibration energy. Often worn in ancient times as a talisman against curses, it will dispel any illusions about what you think you want and guide you towards what you really need, and is useful for resolving internal conflict.

A good guide on using your power with integrity, tiger's eye can help you to understand your talents and abilities and accomplish goals with a clear vision. A healer of self-worth, it dissolves self-criticism while showing you any faults that need to be conquered.

Tiger's eye lifts the mood and is a great stone for blocked creativity.

- **Appearance:** Brown-yellow, red, pink, blue. Small, tumbled, banded.
- **Mohs scale hardness:** 6.5–7
- **Associated chakras:** The most common variety, the brown-yellow tiger's eye, is associated with the lower chakras – root, sacral and solar plexus.
- **Additional tips for use:** When placed on the third eye, tiger's eye can facilitate the rise of kundalini energy from the lower chakras. Placed on the solar plexus, it can ground scattered energies.

ONYX

The strength-giving onyx comes most often as either a black or banded stone, and takes its name from the Greek *onux* meaning "nail" or "claw". Cupid is alleged to have clipped the nails of Venus while she slept, with the clippings turning into onyx. This gem imbues the wearer with mental strength, fortitude and stamina, and brings out the ability to take charge of one's destiny.

It's a supportive stone for tricky circumstances – it eliminates worries, and comforts during times of severe mental or physical stress. It centres your energy, aligning you with the Divine and helping you to learn your Earthly lessons.

Helping you to make wise decisions, it enhances self-control and can be stabilizing for those with flighty tendencies.

- **Appearance:** Black, brown, blue, yellow, red, grey, white. All sizes. Polished, banded, marble-like.
- **Mohs scale hardness:** 6.5–7
- **Associated chakras:** All
- **Fun fact:** Onyx is a popular worry stone in the Middle East – people rub the stone between their fingers for a soothing effect. Some believe onyx aids recovery from a past relationship or unrequited love.

BIRTHSTONES

There are birthstones for every month of the year, and wearing your special crystal is believed to enhance health, happiness and prosperity not just in your birthday month, but all year round! Discover your birthstone in the next chapter – it's a great excuse to wear a stunning piece of jewellery and celebrate your birthday every day!

Let nothing bind you in the world other than your highest inner truth.

EMMA HERWEGH

January
GARNET

Garnet comes in many types and colours, with red and brown (almandine) being the most popular. Each type comes with its own additional properties, but they all provide strength, courage and hope. In ancient times, this crystal was carried as a protective talisman.

Garnets are powerful regenerators, capable of balancing energy and bringing either serenity or passion, whatever is appropriate to the situation! They can also help with removing taboos and dissolving old patterns. As an added bonus, garnets are believed to balance the sex drive, and inspire love and devotion. You may want a few of these stones hanging around!

- **Appearance:** Brown, black, red, yellow, orange, green, pink. Transparent to opaque, any size.
- **Mohs scale hardness:** 6.5–7.5
- **Associated chakras:** All, depending on type
- **Additional tips for use:** Place on the third eye for past life recall.

February

AMETHYST

Nature's natural tranquilliser, this beautiful stone calms, soothes and mops your brow! Useful for grief, anxiety and anger it can also soothe you to sleep and ease tension and headaches.

Derived from the Greek word *amethustos*, meaning "not intoxicated", it moderates mood and supports in overcoming addictions or blockages.

Amethyst is beneficial for the respiratory and digestive systems and boosts hormone production, helping to regulate the endocrine system. It can be a comforting stone for those about to transition through death. This highly spiritual stone enhances intuition and psychic gifts.

- **Appearance:** Purple/lavender. Clear, often pointed crystals. All sizes.

- **Mohs scale hardness:** 7

- **Associated chakras:** Crown

- **Care instructions:** Fades in sunlight. Should not be used by those experiencing paranoia or schizophrenia.

- **Fun fact:** Once worn to prevent drunkenness, it can sober you up from overindulgence and physical passions!

March

AQUAMARINE

This beautiful aqua-green stone is strongly connected to water energy and is often called the gem of the sea. Its name derives from the Latin *aqua* – "water" – and *marina* – "of the sea". In ancient times, it was carried by sailors to protect them from drowning.

The soothing waves of the aquamarine can cool the hottest of tempers and melt away stress, leaving a calm mind and a clean aura. Its gentle rays clear pathways of communication, assisting in public speaking or performance. Ideal for ailments involving the throat or thyroid, this zen stone facilitates closure and brings rejuvenation to the mind, body and spirit.

- **Appearance:** Clear or opaque, small, tumbled.
- **Mohs scale hardness:** 7.5–8
- **Associated chakras:** Throat
- **Fun fact:** In the Middle Ages, aquamarine was thought to be excellent for seeing into the future – it was a popular choice for crystal balls!

April

DIAMOND

Who doesn't love this beautiful jewel? It's expensive, hard as nails and survives everything, as well as being dazzlingly beautiful. It symbolizes purity, love and commitment, bringing strength and clarity into the life of the wearer and attracting abundance.

Diamond also amplifies energy, and its searing light can highlight anything that requires transformation, bringing new beginnings. This crystal's ability to allow the light of your soul to shine will make diamond your best friend.

- **Appearance:** White; also blue, yellow, pink, brown. Small, transparent.
- **Mohs scale hardness:** 10
- **Associated chakras:** Crown
- **Care instructions:** None. Diamond is the hardest known mineral. Scratch away!
- **Fun fact:** The ancient Romans believed diamonds were pieces of stars that had fallen to Earth.

May

EMERALD

Emerald is known as the stone of inspiration, infinite patience and successful love. A life-affirming mineral, it's said to enhance domestic bliss, loyalty and unconditional love in both partnership and friendship. This lovely stone promotes truth and wisdom, having a calming effect on the wearer and helping to overcome any misfortune. The colour of spring, emerald is believed to aid regeneration and recovery, and assist with the healing of malignant illnesses and claustrophobia. It's even been used as an antidote to poisons. If emerald changes colour, it's said to warn of unfaithfulness.

- **Appearance:** Small and bright when polished; larger ones tend to be raw and cloudy.
- **Mohs scale hardness:** 7.5–8
- **Associated chakras:** Heart
- **Care instructions:** Can trigger negative emotions if worn continuously.
- **Fun fact:** Emerald was once thought to protect the wearer from magicians' tricks. Emerald was also the stone of the goddess Venus.

June

PEARL

Known to be associated with wisdom, these serene little gems also symbolize purity, loyalty and integrity, attracting good luck and abundance. Pearls can bring truth to the surface, boost fertility and ease pain and discomfort in childbirth. Natural pearls are rare and most are cultured with the intervention of man.

- **Appearance:** Usually white or cream, but can be any colour; small. Man-made ones are likely to be round and identical with a glassy look, while real or cultured pearls are likely to be irregularly shaped with a hint of green or pink translucent lustre.
- **Mohs scale hardness:** 2.5
- **Associated chakras:** Root, heart, third eye, crown
- **Care instructions:** Pearls are soft and scratch easily. Never store them in a plastic bag, as chemicals found in plastic can damage their surface.

July

RUBY

Often considered the gemstone of royalty, dynamic ruby is associated with sun energy and stimulates life-force and passion. It takes its name from the Latin *ruber*, meaning "red", and it clears negative energy and anger, opening and balancing the heart. Ruby is a stone of abundance and helps you to retain wealth in all areas. Highly protective, it also promotes courage and strength, enhancing leadership qualities and sharpening the mind. Its high vibrational energy is beneficial for the heart and circulatory system.

- **Appearance:** Red. Small, bright and transparent polished; otherwise larger and opaque.
- **Mohs scale hardness:** 9
- **Associated chakras:** Heart
- **Additional tips for use:** Can overstimulate in sensitive people.
- **Fun fact:** Burmese warriors believed that the ruby made them invincible in battle. Some ancient cultures believed that rubies grew on trees like fruit, turning red when ripened.

August

PERIDOT

Peridot takes its name from the Old French *peritot*, meaning "gold". A powerful cleanser, this visionary stone clears debris from the past and supports clear thinking and spiritual truth. Also able to alleviate jealousy, resentment and anger, it promotes healthy self-esteem, improves difficult relationships and helps you to forgive your own mistakes.

- **Appearance:** Small; olive or yellowy-green, honey, brown, red. Opaque; clear when polished.
- **Mohs scale hardness:** 6.5–7
- **Associated chakras:** Heart, solar plexus
- **Care instructions:** Rapid or uneven heat can cause fracture.
- **Fun fact:** Peridot is thought to be as old as our solar system. Back on Earth, it is often found in meteor craters, earning it the name "the extra-terrestrial gemstone".

September
SAPPHIRE

Known as the wisdom stone, the name sapphire comes from the Latin *saphirus* and the Greek *sapheiros*, both meaning "blue". Sapphires come in several colours but blue is the most popular, although each has its own type of knowledge to reveal.

In general, it focuses and calms the mind, releasing unwanted thoughts and freeing the wearer from depression and spiritual confusion. Good at attracting prosperity, it is believed to help with conditions of the eyes and blood, calms overactive body systems and regulates glands. Blue sapphire is associated with spiritual truth and romantic love.

- **Appearance:** Blue, black, purple, green, yellow. Small and bright (polished), or large and opaque (raw).

- **Mohs scale hardness:** 9

- **Associated chakras:** Throat

- **Additional tips for use:** Can release frustration and aid self-expression when placed or worn at the throat.

- **Fun fact:** Rulers of ancient Persia believed the sky to be blue because it was reflecting the colour of sapphire stones.

October

OPAL

The name opal derives from the Sanskrit *upala*, or "precious stone", and the Greek *opallios*, "to see a change of colour". This delicate crystal is a stone of emotion and reflects the wearer's mood. It can amplify emotions, bringing them to the surface for conscious transformation. Linked with love and passion, the sensual opal supports spontaneity and loyalty but may amplify existing fickleness.

Opal promotes zest for life, creativity, self-expression and self-esteem and wants to help the wearer to reach their true potential.

- **Appearance:** Small, polished. Various colours and lustres.

- **Mohs scale hardness:** 5.5–6.5

- **Associated chakras:** Various, depending on type

- **Care instructions:** Opal is delicate so be careful not to break or chip it.

- **Fun fact:** Romans often gave opal amulets to their wives for protection and good fortune.

November

TOPAZ

Known as the stone of love and good fortune, the empathetic topaz soothes, stimulates and motivates, helping you to successfully achieve your goals. Ancient Egyptians believed topaz was coloured by the glow of the sun god, Ra, and this stone's vibrant energy will help you spread joy and sunshine. It pierces through doubt, promoting trust in the universe and supporting honesty, forgiveness and self-realization.

A superb emotional support stone, topaz calms emotions and helps the wearer to be receptive to love of all kinds – bring it on!

- **Appearance:** Blue, golden-yellow, clear, green, brown, red-pink. Transparent, small and faceted to large.
- **Mohs scale hardness:** 8
- **Associated chakras:** Various
- **Fun fact:** The largest faceted gemstone in the world is the El Dorado topaz, mined in Brazil in 1984. It weighs 31,000 carats and is a beautiful pale yellow-brown. The topaz crystalline structure is very stable, allowing it to produce very large crystals.

December
TANZANITE

This high vibration stone is good for beginners in psychic communication, allowing safe exploration of the higher realms. This makes it an excellent choice for deep meditation and spiritual development.

Tanzanite is also a good crystal for those considering a career change, and can help with finding your true vocation. If you feel over-worked, tanzanite will balance your energy and help you to find time for yourself. As well as being useful for depression and anxiety, tanzanite can resolve head–heart conflicts, and supports a compassionate heart and enlightened mind.

- **Appearance:** Violet-blue. Small. Polished, slightly opaque when raw.
- **Mohs scale hardness:** 6–7
- **Associated chakras:** Throat, third eye, crown
- **Care instructions:** Easily scratched.
- **Fun fact:** Found only in Tanzania, tanzanite is thought to be 1,000 times rarer than diamonds.

LAST WORD

It is clear that each crystal is as unique, mystical and fascinating as the last, and the benefits of having them in your daily life are limitless! With these practical tips on how to care for your crystals and how to best utilize each one, we hope you are able to explore the value of a wide selection of readily available gems. The use of crystals for health benefits – of body, mind and spirit – is knowledge that has been with us since time immemorial, and while public opinion on these natural resources may come and go, their health benefits are always there for us to call upon.

Every crystal has its own unique properties, and each can work with us in different ways. Take time to experiment with some of the crystals in this book and get to know how they work for you. Welcoming crystals in to your world can lead you on a life-long journey of healing, self-discovery and expansion. Every crystal is as unique and beautiful as each one of us.

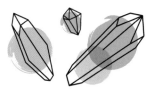

CRYSTAL INDEX

IMAGE CREDITS

Have you enjoyed this book? If so, find us on Facebook at **Summersdale Publishers**, on Twitter at **@Summersdale** and on Instagram at **@summersdalebooks** and get in touch. We'd love to hear from you!

www.summersdale.com